Trellises & Thorns

PAM LASKIN

DOS MADRES

2024

DOS MADRES PRESS INC.
P.O. Box 294, Loveland, Ohio 45140
www.dosmadres.com   editor@dosmadres.com

Dos Madres is dedicated to the belief that the small press is essential to the vitality of contemporary literature as a carrier of the new voice, as well as the older, sometimes forgotten voices of the past. And in an ever more virtual world, to the creation of fine books pleasing to the eye and hand.

Dos Madres is named in honor of Vera Murphy and Libbie Hughes, the "Dos Madres" whose contributions have made this press possible.

Dos Madres Press, Inc. is an Ohio Not For Profit Corporation and a 501 (c) (3) qualified public charity. Contributions are tax deductible.

Executive Editor: Robert J. Murphy

Illustration & Book Design: Elizabeth H. Murphy
www.illusionstudios.net

Cover painting by Elissa Cohen

Typeset in Adobe Garamond Pro & Nuptial BT
ISBN 978-1-953252-99-9
Library of Congress Control Number: 2023951323

ACKNOWLEDGEMENTS

Acknowledgement is made to the following publications in which these poems appeared or will soon be appearing.

Wisteria and Weeds : BIG CITY LIT, 2022
Prayers : JANE'S WALK, 2019
Shared Rooms : MER VOX 18, Winter, 2020
Overgrown Gardens : NYC FROM THE INSIDE,
    Ed. By George Wallace
Broken Wrist, Old Age : POETRY IN PERFORMANCE 50
Waking Up : PROMETHEAN, Spring, 2023
Dandelion : THE WAITING ROOM, Spring, 2023
In Newspaper Sheets : www.acousticlevitation.org

To Friends and Family—
the flowers in my garden—
and to Samantha, my Rose

TABLE OF CONTENTS

I — Weeds & Thorns

II — Trellises

Trellises & Thorns

INTRODUCTION

I cultivate a garden which is filled with flowers—friends and family—all of whom radiate vibrant colors. They anchor me to rich soil. Yet, even with this blossoming, there are weeds—too many which demand to be plucked—Covid; the war in Ukraine; the conflict in the Middle East, and on a personal level—growing old; the body breaking down; the challenges of daily life. My epigraph encapsulates all of this.

I turned to the ghazal to express this dismay, but also because it is such a heart-felt form. The repetition of the second line in the couplet emphasizes the urgency of recreating the world, so it has more trellises than thorns. The ghazal is grounded in song; it is the Greek chorus lamenting too many sorrows. It is a Middle Eastern form, so I imagine it as a form that cries out for peace in that regional area.

Indeed, these poems cry out (sing out!) for justice, civility, decency and ultimately hope. They rise up in prayer, imagine the child will take the seeds and plant a newer, better, different garden. The ultimate message, despite the many thorns, is there is always "The Rose", where: "Sweet smells/ every crevice of my nose/while its colors/excite the eyes."

This is the song my ghazals sing!

Pamela L. Laskin
10/10/2023

Epigraph:

In my Garden

There is always
the rose—
whose smell saturates
every crevice
of my nose,
so sun
spreads
inside,
while its color
excites the eyes
explosion
of senses,
but not to forget
the thorns,
no matter where I touch
I prick and bleed,
you may not see it,
but it's there.

I
Weeds & Thorns

Wisteria and Weeds

Going to grow a gorgeous garden
with wisteria blooming
and roses
ripe with longing.
I had the seeds,
the soil.
All was ripe
for blossoming,
even the way I measured
the distance between where the seeds
were planted.

How could I have known
the heat was venomous,
the waters were dying of thirst,
the sun snuck behind smog;

never did I dream
of the disasters of war
drought
a virus that ravaged
so many lives.

This garden
was futile
destined to die
in parched soil
one that gave birth
to weeds in abundance.

Seeds in September

My mother gave me seeds
to plant a garden—
"wisteria," she says
grow abundant like a forest
purple vines twisting their way
around the belly
of a tree;
I became the family's gardener
planting, watering, praying,
over my mother's rosary,
for abundant sunshine,

never imagining
months later
weeds would grow uncontrollably
in the bombed-out yard,
and my missing father.

Prayers

World War III beckons
precious seeds of peace

daily hungry children cry
precious seeds of peace

hungry Mamas soon will die
precious seeds of peace

broken homes destroyed by bombs
precious seeds of peace

mass graves building mountains
prayers for seeds of peace.

Trying to Write About Ukraine

This morning arms can't move
my roots have died.

I try to grasp a pen to write
but roots have died,

instead I watch the morning news
these roots have died

kindness now an after-thought
such roots have died

this grief it grows a grotesque tree
whose roots have died

Ukrainians they daily flee
a rootless world, that's died.

Write/Right

Nine hundred bodies in mass graves
not mine to write,

daily children orphaned
not mine to write

severed arms and severed limbs
can't ever write

a child's cry for Mama
can't ever write

buildings burn in blazing fire
how to write

Mamas and their babies leave
Dad's left to fight

watching towns bereft of food
water, warmth—not right.

Coronavirus, 2020

The city has shut down
it is a plague,

my body undercover
sleeps in plagues

grief grows like a garden
of gangrened plagues

daily virus blooms
like any plague

the elderly are victims
they die in plagues

I try to stay inside
in hell I'm plagued

better than to die
and be the plague.

Covid, 2021

My house is filled with fake plants
since they don't die

the leaves are green and radiant
they never die

I do not have to water them
they will not die

they think of me a botanist
they never die

with other shrubs my thumb is black
they always die

more than half a million dead
they all have died.

Marigold

The delta variant spreads its venom
I weave it into gold,

so many died, dead like flies
must weave it into gold

when guns go haywire in the streets
I weave it into gold

what writers do when grief just grows
we weave it into gold

this doesn't make a happy poem
when weaving into gold

wanton words of marigolds
growing into gold.

Begonia

I know the secrets of the heart
begonias bursting

instinct tells me sorrow grows
begonias bursting

I try to plant in perfect rows
begonias bursting

cannot heal the lives now lost
begonias bursting

my garden's here for you to grow
begonias bursting.

Queen Anne's Lace: Sanctuary

For every child who lost a parent
my garden is yours to hide in

the bullets fly like confetti
my garden is yours to hide in

you sleep on the corner without any shoes
my body is yours to hide in

sheltering, shielding sorrow on skin
my body is yours to hide in

refuge from grief, Queen Anne's lace
plenty of garden to hide in.

Black-Eyed Susan

Witness the woman wearing no shoes
I am the black-eyed Susan

politicians do not follow rules
I am the black-eyed Susan

gazing with only one black eye
since that is the black-eyed Susan

daily children at borders, they die
I am the black-eyed Susan

since I can see with clarity
being the black-eyed Susan

begging my children to help mend this world
says Mama, black-eyed Susan.

Waking Up

Lately
I've spent so much time
kvetching
about politics
cold
the masks
getting old

when the pandemic
is a shawl
chronically worn
never admired,

I forgot to tell you
I have a class;
cherished students
who smile on Zoom
like they are auditioning a life
I thought had passed me by.

They are radiant
because I told a joke
made them laugh
while my grandchildren
burrow in my skin
like summer
in October;

tomorrow
is Halloween
some mean trick
to have a virus
that never heard
of social distancing
spread its venom
in every unmasked crevice,

yet
there is still the treat
(small, it may seem)
of waking up
every day.

Gladiolus

To Doris

I weep for my students who hide
stand strong as the gladiolus

a year when so many have died
stand strong as the gladiolus

my children are grounded in grief
stand strong as the gladiolus

I cherish each line on a leaf
hold tight to my strong gladiolus

yet times I can't bear such a chore
stand strong as this gladiolus

life tells me I must do more
to keep strong my heart's gladiolus.

Zinnia

Solitary in your soil
your zinnia is broken

too many grieving gone this year
your zinnia is broken

recall you were the one who healed
other broken zinnias

a million lives lost this year
buried zinnias in the garden

there is a heart of healing
in your garden of zinnias

your flower knows growth is hard
this zinnia need not be broken

mending a melody of different flowers
blossom out of broken.

Age

My nightmares awaken
in a gnarled tree

this body, it's forsaken
in a gnarled tree

my finger branches bent
like a gnarled tree

my breathing often spent
with this gnarled tree

I try to climb the top
of this gnarled tree

but every time I stop
this old, gnarled tree.

Broken Wrist, January 2022

My arm a broken trunk
off on the side of the road

the pain of these gnarled branches
off on the side of the road

there are no leaves to give you
off on the side of the road

the years they can deceive you
off on the side of the road

they say it will get better
off on the side of the road

as rains are getting wetter
off on the side of the road

and trees continue falling
in forest and on roads.

Gardens of Ghazals

Every day I fight
I hide in the garden of ghazals

Coronavirus blight
aside from the garden of ghazals

murders in plain sight
but not in the garden of ghazals

the world is still not right
but blooms in the garden of ghazals

very little light
except in the garden of ghazals

so every day I write
to help grow this garden of ghazals.

Gaza/Israel

I want to pollinate
but this garden's filled with thorns

wedded to your weeds
your garden's filled with thorns

what's wrong with planting primroses
your garden's filled with thorns;

or watering abundantly
your garden's filled with thorns;

I wanted to have flowers
but was challenged by your thorns

such hate grows by the hour
in this garden filled with thorns.

Sorry, No Money

His gums are bleeding every day
our country has no money.

He cries before he makes it home
our country has no money.

Age seven and he's free to roam
our country has no money.

He finds a mushroom on the ground
our country has no money.

Hunger haunts him all around
our country has no money,

so when he eats a poisoned fruit
this country has no money.

Can look into the pit of grief
say sorry, there's no money.

In Newspaper Sheets

So many boys dead on the street
mama's cry out for babies around
cover their faces with newspaper sheets.

So many people suffer from heat
bodies in freezers weeping with sound
too many people die on the streets.

Virus and guns haunting the street
violence a plague that's keeping us bound
so many stories in newspaper sheets.

Grief is a ghost setting the beat
sorrow a skin that falls to the ground
so many children dead on the street.

Piles of bodies, sorrow a feat
daily it grows a mountainous mound
cannot be covered by just a sheet
too many people dead on the street.

Hands of Grief

The song I sing has lost its tune
replaced by sorrow

the trees are all bereft of leaves
they bend in sorrow

the sky is always winter blue
clouds float with sorrow

the dreams I had, now so few
aside from sorrow

I look upon your empty face
entrenched in sorrow

the body's casket cannot move
it's filled with sorrow.

Dandelion

To Ruth

The wind is wild with heavy weight
blow wishes on this dandelion

the gun-craze grows, dormant hate
blow wishes on this dandelion

Covid spreads like wildfire
blow wishes on this dandelion

the death-toll spikes, dread is dire
blow wishes on this dandelion

I try to weed the seeds of sorrow
blow wishes on this dandelion

to parachute new dreams tomorrow
scattered wishes, dandelion.

Humpty Dumpty Revisited

Last year
drowned in darkness
where it will stay, hopefully
nothing but a faint memory
of a world
Humpty Dumpty could never fix,

so I look
to the year ahead
when I awaken
to children with full stomachs
people with beds to sleep on
heat when it is below freezing,

with hope
of exiting the tornado of a tunnel
where the pieces, one by one
can be put together
safely again.

II

Trellises

The Garden

To Addie

The soil is your body
your garden grows

this year the flowers cowered
yet your garden grows

it's weathered wild storms
your garden grows

such succulents take form
your gardens grows

and me, I'm not a planter
but I watch your garden grow

I linger with your flowers
forever, gardens grow.

Sunflower

To Janet

You have stood
forever in my garden
strong, sturdy
your dark center
a magnet
for every gazing eye,

the sun
of yellow petals
an umbrella
of protection.

A Finished Book

To Mom, Gladys

You embraced me, I—a daughter
like in a book

loved family so fiercely
as in a book

the library a garden
beloved books

you traveled many lands
inside your books

found silence and serenity
because of books

also lots of love
from friends—and books

now we say good-bye
but not to books

to the cherished chapters of your life
you built with books.

Flowering

To Ira, Happy Anniversary

I used to grow grief
until I found your garden

you touched a hidden leaf
when I found your garden

got rid of all my weeds
when I found your garden

planted special seeds
when I found your garden

now I reach for sun
when I found your garden

now I reach for sun
linger in your garden

you've always been the one
to embrace me in your garden.

Sweet Smelling Soil

Raised in concrete
I saw your soil

still a weed broke through
concrete, not soil

the weed, it lingered long
I saw your soil

watered very well
to plant in soil

it beckoned me inside
the warmth of soil

gave me a place to hide
such special soil

felt good to grow with you
sweet-smelling soil

a life I never knew
saturated in your soil.

Strong and Sturdy

Your tree
(embedded in my soil)
has such strong roots
that wind can whip—
hurricane strong,
and rains can mercilessly
pour their puny hearts out,
but you will still stand
take the hand
of any weakened leaf,
and guide it
to its sky of protection,
since no storm
could ever
knock you down.

Hiding

To Ira

The day it drowned in clouds
when I hid inside my garden

the flowers seemed like shrouds
when I hid inside my garden

the sun was dormant, too
when I hid inside my garden

beneath the nimbus, you
when I hid inside my garden

you didn't see the weeds
when I hid inside my garden

you offered me your seeds
when I hid inside my garden

I felt some flowers sprout
when I hid inside my garden

and now the seasons shout
no more hiding in this garden.

Hands

To Ira

Married many years
we still hold hands

the tree I call your body
has many hands

you talk about your dreams
dealt a wrong hand

excavations and exploring
not in your hands

the husband and the father
such helpful hands

the depth of your desire
in my heart's hands.

Homes

To Ira

There's always broken windows
inside this home

or a cracked wall
inside this home

the doors do not protect us
inside this home

what door ever does
inside a home

we hope the structure stands
inside this home

the year the heating went
inside this home

your body kept me warm
inside this home

the foundation thwarts all harm
inside this home.

Shared Rooms

For Elissa

You sixteen and me eighteen
we shared a room

college and its chaos
inside our room

graduation, a job, a wedding
in bigger rooms

after came the babies
no longer room

for reams of conversation
or quiet rooms

marriage, sometimes children
found us in ruins

secrets kept in vaults
locked in a room

again, we open house
to our heart's ruin

today another sorrow
invades our room

together we can climb
in our shared room.

Trellises

To Craig, Amanda, Ella, & Jake

Termites tore through the foundation
trellises stood strong

terrific times of great elation
trellises stood strong

you tried to keep the mold away
trellises stood strong

growing gardens every day
trellises stood strong

hard to keep the bugs at bay
trellises stood strong

sometimes rain, sometimes gray
trellises stood strong

still the sun, flowers flowing
trellises stood strong

your home stands, poised with power
trellises stand strong.

Wisteria

Yes,
I am wisteria
I climb
by twining stems
around any available support.

Purple, pink, fragrant
I have found my support
Ukraine
my beautiful country,

my free-flowing form
abundant, lush
has taken root
in your soil;

I'm not
going away.

Gardens

You thought we'd stay buried
you imagined us
six feet under
(and made sure of that, for some),

but many
burst through soil
fantastic phototropism
we rise.

Watch us flower
and pollinate;
gaze at our garden
with its wild, colorful flowers
growing in abundance.

We are not going anywhere.
We are the Ukraine.

In Summer

To Ella

You travel like the wind
with speed in summer

your words leave me behind
with speed in summer

your hugs are always kind
no need in summer

watching you grow tall—
a weed in summer

grow bigger still, with dreams
with speed in summer

joy blossoms and it beams
so blessed in summer.

Baking, A Wedding Poem

To Samantha & Josh

Arrived past midnight light
born a blessing

a flock of happy hands
awakens blessings

creating dreams with words
the bones of blessings

Samantha is our song
that sings of blessings

creating dreams with words
the bones of blessings

now there is her Josh
still more blessings

they heal each other's wounds
bandaged blessings

make each other's sun rise
undress more blessings

respect the other's journey
discover blessings

best friends and sacred soulmates
baking blessings.

Prayers

To Samantha Rose on her 30th

Born as a breath
hands clasped in prayer like a rose

they placed a pink hat—a girl—a surprise
answer to prayers, named you Rose

explorer's eyes, but words were few
secret prayers—the rose of you

searching for snails, for magic and flowers
roses raised in prayer, all blue

your stalk, not tall, but a mind measured
by bouquets of colored roses

engrossed in anatomy, the stamen, the pollen
and prayers of fragrant roses

family first, with bursts and hibernations
dreams of desire that rose

dancing inside abundant gardens
passionate prayers, a rose that grew.

Hyssop: Sacrifice

To Samantha

Purple blossoms, radiant
time to be a flower

I have little pollen left in me
time for you to flower

sometimes leaves are brown at edges
but not for you, my flower

summer has me growing less
not for you, my flower

now ready to stop gardening
you have the seeds, my flower.

Overgrown Garden:
A Love Letter to New York

Dear New York,

I should have left you
when it was easy
could have traipsed
into a spring of sunshine and sparrows
where miles of clean beaches
beautiful sunsets
and the stores
you might take me to
shelved with caviar, Perrier
simple breath
home-baked bread
radiant in light and bright
a costume of white,

still
I allowed you
under my skin
sweat of summer sidewalks
too much garbage
lingering like an open mouth
spewing
a restless mass;
you were gritty and dirty
feverish
without any relief.

At the corner bodega
you bought me a Slushy
and the voices
of language—
English, Spanish, Arabic, Bengali, Hindi—
a meandering queue
of faces and places
made me dizzy
with desire.

New York
your frantic air is stifling
yet you pull me into this frenzy
of taste and smell and color;
how could I ever leave you?

Even the daffodil
loves to linger
in your overgrown garden.

Love, Me

ABOUT THE AUTHOR

 PAMELA L. LASKIN is a lecturer in the English Department at City College, where she teaches undergraduate and graduate Children's Writing, and directs the Poetry Outreach Center. Several of her children's and poetry books have been published. RONIT AND JAMIL, A Palestinian/Israeli ROMEO AND JULIET in verse was published by Harper Collins in 2017, and was named among the 35 books to have on your radar for 2017. BEA, a picture book, was a finalist for the Katherine Paterson Prize for Children's Fiction in 2018. She is the winner of the 2018 International Fiction Prize from Leapfrog Press, and WHY NO BHINE, an epistolary novel about the Rohingya Muslims, was published in 2019. The Operating System published a bilingual picture book, MONSTER MARIA, which is about Hurricane Maria, and is being used as a fundraiser for after-school programs in Puerto Rico. Linus Press published MY SECRET WISH about families seeking asylum, and is also being used as a fundraiser for Immigrant Families Together. Cervena Barva Press just published WORDS UNWHISPERED, her first book of ghazals. THE LOST LANGUAGE OF CRAZY, a middle grade-novel, was published in November, 2021 (Atmosphere Press). She is currently at work with Ukrainian author Vasyl Makhno on a YA novel in verse, WISTERIA AND WEEDS, whose focus is on the war in the Ukraine, and what it means for the lives of teens. Finally, she is this year's (2023) recipient of Judith's Room Freedom Through Literacy Board option prize for her current novel.

Follow her: twitter@RonitandJamil and follow her blog: http://PamelaLaskin.blogspot.com/

Other books by Pam Laskin
published by Dos Madres Press

Plagiarist (2012)

She is also included in:
Realms of the Mothers:
The First Decade of Dos Madres Press - 2016

For the full Dos Madres Press catalog:
www.dosmadres.com